we are only visitors

Also by Daniel Hertz

Swami Hari: I am a simple forest monk

Available in paperback and Kindle
(See www.amazon.com for purchase information.)

Visit the *Swami Hari: I am a simple forest monk* FACEBOOK page.

we are only visitors

DANIEL HERTZ

1/1/14

Michelle + Chris,

Love You Guys!

Happy New Year!

Daniel Hertz

We Are Only Visitors

© 2013 (first edition) by Daniel Hertz

TO CONTACT DANIEL HERTZ
Email: SimpleForestMonk@gmail.com
Website: www.DanielHertzBooks.Wordpress.com

ISBN: 978-149103005-9

Thank you to Ethan, Anya, James,

and all the other visitors to the planet.

(That means you!)

Contents

We are all visitors to this time, this place.
We are just passing through.
Our purpose here is to observe,
to learn, to grow, to love . . .
and then we return home.

AUSTRALIAN ABORIGINAL PROVERB

Foreword

WHETHER we recognize it or not, we are on a journey. A fortunate few understand that this journey is a spiritual one, a quest for meaning and purpose. These fortunate ones invariably become engaged in a spiritual discipline, some religious, some not, but all designed to answer the fundamental questions of: Who am I? Where did I come from? Where am I going? Each individual's path on this journey is unique to that individual. There is only one way—it is your way. And we have to discover that pathway for ourselves.

We Are Only Visitors is a record of one man's journey, but it is a fractal of everyone's journey. A fractal is a small event that contains every element of the whole event. Every spiritual journey is a fractal of the whole journey. The things we learn are the same for each of us even though the circumstances, the lessons we are given, and the methods will be different. The goal of freedom is the same, only the name changes.

It is, literally, a movement from the uniqueness of the ego-self into the universality of the spiritual-Self. This journey, of course, is far from easy. In fact, it costs "not less than everything." We celebrate those who explore the heavens or dive into the deepest trenches of the seas, and we should. These are feats of daring that demand sacrifice, courage, stamina, and persistence that go far beyond the norm. The inward journey is no less a feat, requiring sacrifice, courage, stamina, and persistence, and it is a solitary journey. The dangers we face on this path are the inner dragons, and there is nowhere to hide. And when we try, the gurudeva and/or teacher finds a way to bring us face-to-face with these inner dragons of the mind.

If we honestly face ourselves, the dragons begin to shift, and we are somehow lifted into realms of joy, contentment, and awareness that are not only sublime, but strengthen our resolve to continue the task before us. We become aware of our brother and sister travelers on the same journey, even though they will certainly be on a different path than the one we chose. At a certain point, beliefs, philosophies, even methods, matter little—it is the intention and the desire for freedom that we find in our fellow travelers that inspires us to even greater effort. Some travel far, some travel only a short distance, but uniqueness and individuality fade into the greater embrace of shared spiritual experience, and we learn from our fellow travelers.

In *We Are Only Visitors*, Daniel Hertz shares his journey and insights. They may not be the same as yours, they may not be great revelations to you, but they are a record of his journey, a sharing of his doubts, his insights, his progress, and most important, his love of the journey. As such, it is a fractal of our own journey, and we see ourselves in his experiences and his insights. We recognize ourselves in his stories and poems, and this inspires us to persist in our own journey to freedom. By offering himself, Hertz gives us an opportunity to look again within ourselves, and to recognize that we are truly guests on a remarkable pilgrimage to eternity.

Phil Nuernberger, PhD
HONESDALE, PENNSYLVANIA

Introduction

IN *We Are Only Visitors* we are privileged to follow Daniel on a path through a series of intimate contemplations on many events in his life, thoughts, and spiritual progress. We see a transformation from anxiety over the impermanence of life and the challenge of living with our inevitability of death on "the planet," to a joy and acceptance couched deeply in gratitude for all of it.

The Australian aboriginal proverb, "We are all visitors to this time, this place. We are just passing through. Our purpose here is to observe, to learn, to grow, to love . . . and then we return home," acts as a spiritual underpinning of all of the topics to be explored in Daniel's book.

Each one of us will find ourselves in many of the events, perspectives, fears, and discoveries that are shared. Why? Because what Daniel discusses in the essays and poetry is quintessentially the "human condition."

Daniel's book takes us on a journey of both inside and outside travels, and in the process offers us a gentle questioning and a wisdom concerning many of our own common life situations. He provides, in a very clear and simple way, many sane lessons for living a worthy and loving life and understanding and facing death.

His essays and poems are personal and intimate, and at the same time, one might almost say objective or universal. For example, throughout his writings, he refers to the earth we live on as "the planet," giving the dual perspective of one who lives on the planet, while at the same time, presenting the perspective of an observer reporting on the earth from afar.

I would like to offer some background information about Daniel's spiritual orientation in the book. When he refers to "the Tradition," he is referring to the Himalayan Tradition of Yoga Meditation, which he has practiced for the last twenty years.

The Himalayan Tradition of Yoga Meditation draws from three sources of wisdom: the teachings of the *Yoga Sutras* of Patanjali, the philosophy and practices of the Tantras, and the oral instructions and initiatory experiences passed on by a long line of masters.

A key element of this Tradition is that it does not require adherence to a belief system but experientially helps verify the metaphysical reality. The principal tenets and practices of all known systems of meditation are included in this Himalayan system. For the most part, they have arisen out of it. For example: Buddhist *Vipassana* believes only in breath awareness; Transcendental Meditation believes only in mantra; Hatha Yoga practitioners pay attention mainly to the posture. The Himalayan meditator learns to sit in the correct posture, practices correct breathing and relaxation, and combines mantra with the breath awareness.

It is rare that a disciple can master all of these components of the Himalayan system. But he may master one or two aspects, and be sent out to teach. He will draw the students who are at a level of development where they can benefit from the system he has to offer. When the given student has reached the ultimate end of the methods in the particular subsystem, his next steps will be in the other aspects of the Himalayan system.

These are the chief components of the Himalayan system as espoused by Swami Veda Bharati:

1. Purification of thoughts and emotions
2. Mindfulness
3. Breath awareness, which begins as the very first step in the practice of meditation

WE ARE ONLY VISITORS   *xiii*

4. Calming of the sense faculties by first calming the mind, then with this facility becoming aware of the subtle body and deeper meditational practices
5. Use of mantra meditations and mantra repetition (The science of mantra is based on an understanding of sound vibrations produced by repeated repetition. The ultimate purpose of mantra repetitions (*japa*) is to go into deep silence.)
6. Concentrations and the resultant experiences of concentration
7. Meditation proper, which takes place at the deeper levels of mind leading to
8. Liberation, the state of *satchidananda*, truth, consciousness, bliss

For countless centuries, the Himalayan Tradition has been passed on experientially in an unbroken chain of master-disciple relationships.

Within some elements in his essays, Daniel writes of pivotal masters in the Tradition: Swami Rama of the Himalayas, Swami Veda Bharati, and Swami Hariharananda Bharati (Swami Hari), with whom he had an especially close relationship.

Daniel not only presents his personal experience of the Yoga Meditation Tradition, but also in keeping with the openness of the tradition—having grown up in the Jewish faith, which he also still practices—and knowing much about Buddhism and Christianity, we see places in his writings where they all find a place on his path.

I remember Daniel and Nikki's wedding, which was held outside in the Peace Garden near Lake Harriet Park in Minneapolis. It was officiated by a rabbi and attended by Swami Hari and a Buddhist monk, with friends, many representing these and other cultural origins and religious life ways.

In the poetry and essays in *We Are Only Visitors*, Daniel explores his spiritual practices, sharing one of the fundamental realizations of all spiritual traditions: the impermanence of life, the short time we have as visitors here on Earth. His writing compels us to ask deep questions about our brief stay here. How can we understand it, contemplate it, and ultimately find peace and deal gracefully with it?

After you have thoughtfully read all of Daniel's essays and poems, I suggest that you circle around once again to his first poem, *Walk Softly in the Snow*, which is, you might say, the culminating point that all of his contemplations lead to: "To help heal the world as you heal yourself." This is what Daniel is doing with this simple and candid book. Through his writings he demonstrates a wonderful balance and grace, arrived at through Yoga, Meditation, contemplation, and selfless service offered out of a place, not of fear of impermanence, rather from a place of peace and great gratitude for the way things are.

Throughout, Daniel has offered us, in the most gentle way, the inner questioning, seeking and finding of the balance and loving gratitude that one can give back to the earth, its people in general, close friends and family and to us, the readers of his book. The reader comes into contact with a gentle soul, a questioning soul, a morally good soul, one who after living on "the planet" has shared himself and his "way" with us and thereby enriched our understanding. He has shown us what is possible for each of us.

Dr. Claudia Crawford
Professor of Philosophy and Eastern Religions
North Hennepin Community College
BROOKLYN PARK, MINNESOTA

we are only visitors

Preface

Dear Reader,

I never dreamed a second book would come so soon, if at all. For several months after the first book (*Swami Hari: I am a simple forest monk*) came out, I was unable to write anything. No words came out. I honestly did not think I had anything else to say. But then slowly the words started to come and again I became an observer of the process. In the end it became a project that I am really excited about.

Recently someone asked me if we were doing any more fundraising projects for SRIVERM, the school in the remote Himalayas founded by Swami Hari. The answer was no, and that's when it hit me. The new essays and poems were adding up, so why not make another book and, like we did with the first book, donate all the profits to SRIVERM?

Like most things, of course, it is easier said than done. At first, simply trying to reach someone by email at the remote site of SRIVERM became a daunting task. I later found out that their internet had been down for the last seven months. But given the complexities of coordinating a project like this, it went surprisingly smoothly. Every time I became discouraged, someone would offer a word of support and encouragement, and it helped keep me going. Many times I asked myself why am I doing this, and every time this answer came back: Why not?

There are two new Swami Hari-related essays in this book. "Back to India" recounts my twenty-six night stay in Tarkeshwar, the remarkable holy Shiva shrine in the high Himalayan foothills. The previously unpublished excerpts from Swami Hari's lectures and the letters from the students at SRIVERM were not in the original plans, but along the way the idea came to include them in the book. They quickly became the heart and soul of the whole project. The other essays and poems are again rooted in my Yoga practice and cover the topics that are most on my mind: forgiveness, gratitude, birth, death, meditation, nature, attachment, and the mind-body relationship. They are my attempt to try and make sense of a seemingly senseless world.

Several of the essays have previously been published in the *AHYMSIN Newsletter* (www.ahymsin.org). Carolyn Hume and Stephan Hodges do a great job every month of putting the newsletter together. Having a place to share the essays inspired me to keep writing.

Like the first book, it took many people to put a project like this together. I was so grateful to find Judy Gilats to design and typeset the book. Mary Bowman-Cline has painted another incredible book cover. Dr. Phil Nuernberger, a well-respected Yogi and author, quickly agreed to write the foreword. It was a real shot of enthusiasm for the project. Then Dr. Claudia Crawford wrote a great introduction. I hope what she wrote will help give readers a wider perspective on the topics in the book. Jason Hertz and Nandini Avery performed the critical piece of proofreading the book. Their expertise was an invaluable contribution. Judy Law made it possible to get the letters from the students at SRIVERM. And the advice of my wife Nikki has again guided the process.

I do not consider myself a "writer," and definitely not a "poet," but as long as the words keep coming out, I will continue to write them down. I humbly offer these pages to you and sincerely hope you enjoy the experience.

All the best and thank you,
Daniel Hertz
MINNEAPOLIS, MINNESOTA, USA
May 15, 2013

Artwork by Mary Bowman-Cline

Walk Softly in the Snow

What more can we ask
From living
Than to die gracefully
To walk softly in the snow
Without leaving footprints
To repair a smashed wine glass
One tiny piece at a time
To build a bridge
That leads others to freedom
To seek the light of justice
When all we can see is a dark room
To heal the world
As you heal yourself

We Are Only Visitors

RECENTLY I was sitting in a booth at my regular lunch spot, waiting for my food to arrive. While watching the diners come and go, the thought came into my mind very clearly and strongly that *we are only visitors to this planet.* We come and go in much the same way as the people in the restaurant. We are guests here for a short time. If you are a guest in someone's house, there are unwritten etiquette rules you would be expected to follow. Similarly, there are unwritten rules we are expected to follow while on our visit to the planet. Following these rules on our visit allows us to live in harmony with the planet and its inhabitants.

Bring a gift. All of us arrive with special gifts to offer our family, friends, society, and the planet. Some are big. Some are small. Some are clear immediately and some take a lifetime to figure out. As we wind our way through life, eventually the gift is revealed. Either way, we all have something unique and great to offer.

Follow the rules set out by the host. Be on your best behavior. Show the proper respect for the other inhabitants of the planet by getting along with others and finding a way to live peacefully.

Offer to help around the house. If you see a way to improve things, join in and show us how things could be done differently and better. This leads to the practice of selfless service and Karma Yoga.

Keep your room clean. Take care of the environment. Find a way to live that allows future generations to have healthy and prosperous lives.

Do not overstay your welcome. When our time is up on the planet, we need to leave. We don't know when or how. All we know is that one day we will disappear.

Write a thank you note. The key to joyful living is to have an attitude of gratitude. Staying positive and acknowledging what we have allows us to live a more purposeful, conscious, and spiritual life.

There are unending examples of what our host is constantly trying to teach us. One example fresh in my mind comes from a Minnesota snowstorm. This year the winter seemed like it would never end because of three unusually big snowfalls in April. This morning, on April 23, 2013, there was six inches of new snow on the ground when my wife and I woke up. As I looked outside and saw the trees and everything else covered with a thick layer of snow, it seemed incomprehensible that all of it would ever disappear. But with a sunny day and temperatures reaching 40 degrees F, most of the snow was gone by 4:00 PM. Such a major transformation in less than ten hours seemed like nothing short of a miracle. Nature again showed me that anything is possible. It demonstrated again that something beyond our wildest imagination can happen in the blink of an eye.

Sometimes, especially when we are young and healthy, it seems like our visit to the planet will go on forever. But it is actually very short. This is easier to see when we understand that the planet has existed for 4.5 billion years. A 100-year lifespan becomes miniscule. Our life can seem big and permanent, but it is only temporary. The permanency is an illusion, but that is easy to forget when we are going about our everyday living routines. We become immersed in our lives and may only occasionally have the time or desire to contemplate the larger picture.

Here is another way to look at the larger picture. The website www.worldometers.info is constantly, in real time, updating the amount of births, deaths, and many other statistics. For example, on 11:58 AM on April 19, 2013, the world population was 7,111,383,077. As you look at the website you can see this number is constantly increasing. On the same day and time, worldwide, there had already been over 181,561 births and 77,563 deaths. This is also constantly changing. With every new birth and death, the world becomes a little different place in a way that no one can really comprehend. During our visit we have changed the planet in some way.

One day the visit to the planet will end for all of us. While I am here, I am trying my best to be a good guest and follow all the etiquette rules. Maybe I'll be invited back. ❧

10,000 Years

10,000 years from now
Closer than we think
If someone who is
Close to 100 years old
Passes on a message
To a new born baby
And then when that baby
Grows old and
Is close to 100
He or she would pass on
The same message
To another new born baby
And so on
Only 100 people
Who live for 100 years
And a message has been
Passed along
10,000 years into the future

A Message to Pass On

WHILE browsing the web recently I came across a book by Ira Byock, M.D., entitled *The Four Things That Matter Most*. On Amazon I sneaked a peak at the first page and found the four things he is referring to in the title of the book:

1. *Please forgive me.*
2. *I forgive you.*
3. *Thank you.*
4. *I love you.*

I never read his book, but I was struck by how profound these 11 words are. They keep coming back to me, almost like a mantra or prayer. The concepts of forgiveness, love, and gratitude are ordinary human feelings. They are so simple and basic, yet our busy minds can make them so complicated. How you look at them depends on where you are in your life, relationships, and spiritual practice. But wherever you find yourself in life, these words are powerful. They are arguably as powerful as any words we can use. They can change relationships in a moment, and heal and lighten our heart in the process. How can you go wrong by using these words?

These 11 words seem like the perfect guide to living a life. One or more of these four sentences applies to almost everything we do. It is easy to demonstrate this by trying a simple experiment. The next time you are in a difficult and challenging situation, ask yourself which of these words could I say right now to resolve the inner or outer conflict? Saying one of these four simple sentences to yourself or someone else could put you on the road to resolving the issue. It soft-ens the situation and takes the bite out of whatever thoughts are in your mind or whatever comments you have made. If you forgive someone else, it is a great gift for both of you. It helps both people move to a more peaceful and harmonious thought pattern.

I often think of how important these 11 words are and how helpful they could be to people as they move through the journey of life and death. When I say these words, I always feel very humble and grateful. They remind me of how frag-ile life is and how often we stumble along and make mistakes, even if we don't realize it at the time. It also reminds me of all the times I may have unintentionally offended someone. It is a way of telling people: I am human and therefore make mistakes, so I hope you understand. I love you no matter what and thank you for being you. These 11 words can be used often in our daily life and we do not have to wait for a major event to remember them. Forgiveness, cultivating love, and giving thanks have all been well researched. They have clearly been shown to increase health and happiness. I have discovered that there is even an International Forgive-ness Institute, with lots of great information on how to for-give and its benefits. Also, the eighth step in the twelve steps of Alcoholics Anonymous is about asking for forgiveness.

Many world religions include teachings on the nature of forgiveness. What is less clear is if we are asking for divine or human forgiveness. We may never be able to separate those, but whatever the perspective of a particular person, the re-sult is often the same. During the ten-day period of time between Rosh Hashanah and Yom Kippur, it is customary in the Jewish tradition to apologize and ask forgiveness to anyone you may have knowingly or unknowingly offended. This is a very powerful practice. In the times I have tried it, I found that it is very much appreciated by most people. Examples like this can easily be found in many other reli-gions. In the Sermon on the Mount, Jesus repeatedly spoke of forgiveness. In Buddhism, it is critical to forgive oneself and others and cultivate an attitude of loving kindness as you are practicing Meditation.

One of the most profound events in my life was the death of my mother. She died of a short, intense illness that took about three months from diagnosis to death. In the middle of this intense illness she told me this: "No matter what has happened in the past or what will happen in the future, remember that I forgive you and that I love you." At the time she said it, it did not strike me as something especially profound. It was after she died and the finality of death settled in that I realized the importance of what she said. I think she knew how important this would be for me based on how she felt after her own mother had passed away.

Years later, I finally realized those words my mother said to me have turned out to be the most important thing that she left me. They were more important than furniture, money, or other material things (although those are also nice). Many times after her death I felt guilty about things I said or did not say or things I did or did not do. In the grieving process, this can drive a person crazy. But then I thought of those words she said and they helped me a lot. They helped me to move beyond the guilt to the positive memories and loving feelings that those words invoked. They reminded me that she loved me and would want me to be happy and live a fulfilling life. If I had a chance to pass on one message that would give others the same gift as my mother gave me, it would be the 11 words. ⌣

Saying Good-bye

How do you say good-bye
When you don't know how to thank someone

How do you say good-bye
When you don't know what it all means

How do you say good-bye
When you don't know how much someone means to
You until long after they are gone

How do you say good-bye
When many years have passed since their death

How do you say good-bye
When they can no longer hear you

How do you say good-bye
When the only thing you hear in return is silence

How do you say good-bye
When the love comes welling up inside

How do you say good-bye
When you realize the sacrifice someone has made for you

How do you say good-bye

We Are Not the Body

I had heard and read it many times: *We are not the body*. I thought it was clear and that I understood it. It was explained to me like this: If you cut off your hand, are you still you? If you cut off your hand, arm, and leg, are you still you? This goes on and on until eventually your whole body is gone. Then what is left? It goes back to the old meditative question: *Who am I?* Remember the response God gave Moses (Exodus 3:14) when he asked what his name was? It is one of the most famous verses in the Torah. Translated into English from Hebrew, God replied to Moses, *I Am that I Am*.

Last fall, a friend of mine, Vimala Chaitanya, from The Meditation Center, passed away in a hospice situation. On two occasions near the end of her life, even though she was very sick and bedridden, she looked me solidly in the eyes as I was leaving her room and said, "Namaste." Her eyes were illuminated in a very unusual way, almost like the eyes of a cat at night. At the time it felt like she was trying to tell me something but couldn't express it in words. Shortly after that she passed away. The day after her memorial service I felt like I received a direct message from her. This is how it happened:

At 10:00 PM on a quiet, chilly, late October Sunday night in Minneapolis, I had to take my wife Nikki to the urgent care at the hospital. The day before she had injured her foot and it still bothered her. The doctor on call at the urgent care ordered an x-ray. The hospital was deserted and I waited alone for her outside the x-ray room. As I waited, I unexpectedly observed this thought running through my mind,

"I am not afraid of anything in this hospital." For the first time, I realized that the two biggest fears I had about being in a hospital had lost their grip on me. I had a brain MRI and a double hernia operation in the same year, a couple of years ago. The claustrophobia of the MRI machine and the thought of being put to sleep for an operation were almost too much for me to bear at the time. But now, as I sat in the quiet, dimly lit waiting room, a sense of peace came over me.

It turned Nikki she had a fracture in the fifth metatarsal of her left foot. She got her walking boot and crutches and waited in the lobby for me to pick her up. On the way to the car I looked up into the dark sky and saw the brightly illuminated full moon. That is when the message I attribute to Vimala came streaming into my mind: *We are not the body*. I also realized in a much different way than ever before that when we pass away, we leave every last thing behind that we own, including our body. It became clearer to me that we are only temporary visitors to this planet. When our time is up we leave behind everything that seemed so important to us. All those things that we once cherished lose their importance as we let go of our attachment to them. We can let go voluntarily. If not, it is forced on us. We are required to leave it all behind. At some point the physical world simply and utterly loses its meaning.

After a few moments of staring at the moon I continued walking to the car and was jarred back into the reality of having to drive home. It is now several months later and the thought, which was so strong on that moonlit night, has faded away, but the memory still gently lingers.

The Measure of a Life

The wealth accumulated
Or the love given away

The notable accomplishments
Or the sincerity of effort

The fame achieved
Or the friends made along the way

The need to be right
Or doing the right thing

From Simple Forest Monk
to World Traveler

SWAMI Hariharananda Bharati (Swami Hari) called himself a "simple forest monk." He grew up in Toli, the same village as his great uncle, Swami Rama of the Himalayas. They were fifteen years apart in age and never lived in Toli at the same time. But that didn't stop Swami Hari from pursuing Swami Rama for forty-five years. Over the course of that time Swami Rama refused to accept him as a student on nine different occasions. Then one time, without warning, Swami Rama showed up in the middle of the night in Tarkeshwar, the holy Shiva shrine in the Himalayas, to initiate Swami Hari as a monk in the Himalayan Tradition.

I first met Swami Hari in 1998 at the Sadhana Mandir Ashram in Rishikesh. This was my first trip to India. Swami Hari had just come down from Tarkeshwar after twelve years of intensive Meditation practice. His health forced him to retreat from Tarkeshwar's elevation and harsh winters. This proved to be a gift for the rest of the world who had a chance to meet him. We became friends very quickly and had the good fortune to spend a lot of time together in India. Eventually Swami Hari left India and traveled to Minneapolis, Minnesota, to receive medical treatment. I was living in Minneapolis at the time, and our friendship continued to grow. Since both my parents were deceased, Swami Hari saw it as his responsibility to arrange my marriage. Eventually, after seven years of trying, he succeeded in finding me a wife. In the 2011 book, *Swami Hari: I am a simple forest monk,* I tell this story and many others about Swami Hari and the lessons I learned from him.

Over the eight summers he traveled, he kept branching out farther and farther until he had "brothers and sisters" all over the world. Swami Veda Bharati supported him in the beginning of this process and introduced him to many of the Tradition's centers.

Through donations he received, eventually Swami Hari built what he called the Swami Rama Institute of Vocational Education and Research, Malethi (SRIVERM). It is located in the same general area as both Toli and Tarkeshwar. In fact, when standing on the balcony of the guest house at SRIVERM, you can look through the stunningly beautiful valley and see Tarkeshwar. It became a multi-million-dollar project that serves the remote mountain communities in the area. Currently there is a school for grades K-8 with plans to expand a grade each year, a vocational school that trains men and women in plumbing, electricity, computers, sewing, and more, an herbal garden, and a recently certified College of Education training facility. The project has already done amazing work and the potential is enormous.

When Swami Hari passed away in 2008, the fundraising for SRIVERM slowed down quite a bit, but the expenses remained. To help with the fundraising, all book profits from *Swami Hari: I am a simple forest monk* and this book, *We Are Only Visitors,* go directly to SRIVERM. ∽

Excerpts from Lectures
Given by Swami Hari*

DURING the course of writing the book, Nandini Avery of St. Paul, Minnesota, offered transcriptions of some of the previously unpublished lectures by Swami Hari. These excerpts should be helpful for people wanting to learn more about the Simple Forest Monk.

Lecture Excerpt by Swami Hari
SUMMER, 2004

What is this truth? What are the East and West? They are two concepts. In the East people travel inside. In the West people travel outside. Science is the outside journey. There is also the inner journey of human being. If we silently go inside, you can understand all the scripture of the world. These learned people have written certain things. Man was born in the forest. He was completely naked with no clothing at all. He has not brought any books with him. From heaven, no library with him. Today we have many, many libraries in our cities. We have many, many thinkers. There are about more than three hundred religions in this world. Where did these religions come from? Where did these libraries come from? Where did these universities come from? Is this not a

---

*Thanks to Connie Hinnerichs of St. Paul, Minnesota, for transcribing the lectures. Please note that the transcripts have been edited for purposes of clarity and readability.

mystery? Life is itself a mystery, I think. Life is itself a book. The first and last pages of this book are missing. Where did he come from and where will he go?

You have no need to pay anything for this breath. This is freely given to you by nature. If you know how to cultivate this breath, how to make the best use of this breath—inhalation and exhalation—you can achieve great, great things in you. You can achieve enlightenment. You will start knowing what this reality is, what this truth is, what you have come here for. How these books came here. How these universities came here. Who wrote these books? Today, religions, all religions claim these books were written by God. I am telling you God has no time to write any book. Our ancestors have written all these holy books, and today we are fighting to say this or that book is right. This is just like a journey to claim a mountain. You are going to the mountain and there are many, many ways to get to there, and still you have not been to the top. You are fighting to say this or that way is correct. This way is correct. That way is correct. The day you reach the top of the mountain you will see yourself with love. All ways are correct. I am telling you this is the message of Swami Rama. And there you will relax, and that will be your achievement.

And simply doing this Yoga practice, sitting in the corner of your house is enough. You have no need to do many, many efforts. Simple sitting. Simple sitting. And if you can simply sit, go inside and start centering. Ask yourself who you are? Go inside. Ask this question. But this question should be a burning question of yours. Certainly the answer will come. You are this. And this your whole journey becomes. For that, believe me I am not against these books. I am not against any religion. My Guru always says, "You are a living sign of God. Find out within you." And the day you find this out, you will realize he is within you.

Here is a very fine story.

Once a monk went to his teacher and he said, "I want to

know the reality. I want to know the God. I want to know Brahman."

His teacher was very busy. So he said, "Better go to the river and ask a fish. One will come and get you realized. It will get you to know what is God."

At first that monk was surprised. How is it possible that fish will reply? But he knew his teacher was not an ordinary one. He should go.

He went there and stood beside the river, and a very short time later a fish came and it started asking, "Oh man, what do you want?"

That monk was surprised that the fish was speaking human language. Then he got his confidence. If this fish can speak a human language, it means he's an enlightened one.

He said to fish, "My teacher sent me here. He told me a fish would come and let me know what is God, what is Brahman. So since you are speaking I ask you. Will you kindly tell me what is Brahman, what is God?"

This is how the fish replied: "Oh man, I am very, very thirsty since I have not drunk water in many, many years. Will you fetch me a glass of water so that I may quench my thirst? So that I may be brand new?"

That man start thinking how this was possible? This fish lives in the water, but it is thirsty?

He asked, "Oh fish, how it is possible? You are living in water and yet you are thirsty?"

It replied, "Oh man, is this not the answer to your questions? You are living in God and yet you are searching for God?"

Lecture Excerpt by Swami Hari
JULY 7, 2006

Dear brothers and sisters, welcome all of you for this talk. I am not a scholar. I am a simple monk of the forest, and this is imagination. Sometimes I dream I am giving a talk. It's a surprise because now I am here and I am to say something. First I came here to this country and people told me you have to give a talk. I asked, "What is a talk?" Because I did not know that talk is something. But today we will see certain things.

First of all, I want to tell you why I have come. This is a job of mine. A mission to me to tell this country of the old world, that Yoga is a science, not a religion. If anybody says this is a religion, he is fool, nothing else. This is complete science. Science of breath.

Here is a story.

After living and meditating in the forest of Tarkeshwar for many years, one day, late at night, I saw Swami Rama appear outside. It was the month of November. So immediately I jumped and went out the door. I bowed before him.

He said, "I have come here. Tomorrow I am going to initiate you. I am going to take you in my Tradition."

And like this, I became a monk.

That day he told me, "Oh Hari, do you think that I have made you a monk to beg? To go door to door begging? No, I have made you a king of kings."

Sometime a Guru is crazy. (Laughter.) To tell a monk he will become a king of kings? It is impossible, no? But I was keeping mum. That day is gone. In 1995 he gave much work to me.

He said, "Swami Hari, you must go to America."

And he gave many, many jobs to me. I didn't know what is America. Why should I go? But he was my Guru, so I said, "yes, yes, yes." He could say "donkeys," and I would say "yes!" (Laughter.) What could I do? In 1996 he left his body, and because I was a forest man nobody cared for me. Since he was gone from his body, I thought it was impossible that I would ever know about America. But how he has worked!

This institute, which you people have seen in Malethi (SRIVERM), was the dream of my Guru. And he gave that work to me in public. Near about three thousand people were there.

He called me on the stage and said, "Swami Hari will help me build this polytechnic."

And believe me, at the time my position was not to build even a small room. (Laughter.) But when somebody says you will do this in front of three thousand, you cannot say no. And so I said okay. So when he left his body, I thought it would be impossible. I could not do this. All of a sudden he arranged like this that I come to America. I am not a scholar. A forest man, and I am not the master of anything. I used to say I was jack of all, master of none. Now, people started calling me from one place to another. And pretty soon I saw this whole country. I have not seen India as much as I have seen America. California, Dallas, New York, Washington, Honesdale, Buffalo, Milwaukee, Chicago, here, I know, this all. What is this? And like this the technical school started coming into existence. Now I am telling you a very important thing. How did Baba (Swami Rama) manage all these things?

Lecture Excerpt by Swami Hari
AUGUST 16, 2006

My brothers and sisters welcome to you for this talk. Really, you want to meditate? We are searching for peace outside. And peace is within you, within us, not in the market. It's simple, if you really want peace, go inside. And the art of going inside is Meditation.

Again I want to tell you, we have different faces, different bodies, different cultures too. But one thing is common in us, we all breathe. So breathing is most important for us. A child which is not yet born does not breathe. He is not a part of society. A man who is here and not breathing means again he is not part of the society—it means he's dead.

Such a great science, breath, and yet there is no temple of breath in the world. Breath is important. It is no religion. All religions should instruct this breath. Unfortunately, we do not know about breath. Great science. Without breath we cannot survive. And I am telling you this, all of Yoga science teaches about breath. Breath is completely science.

If any Yogi claims that he is Hindu, Muslim, Christian, then he is not a Yogi. A Yogi is he who is only human. When a child is born, he brings no religion with him. We give him religion. If he takes birth in a Hindu family, then a priest will say he is Hindu. If he is born in a Christian family, then the priest will come and say he is Christian. In Islam, the same. And in the name of religion people are fighting. Ah! Jesus told us, Love is God. And many people who believe so-called religion say, gun is God. They want to give us their belief in the name of gun. What is this? Really, if they know the science of breath they will never try to fight. There is no fight if they know the science of breath.

We meditate here daily in the morning. Fortunate are those who come here daily. And one hour, goes, goes, gone. And we say, "Ah! One hour gone?" but you know we have a limitation. After all you have to go to work. But this is a great science of peace. Once you have seen that peace within you I am sure no one would like to disturb that peace. You go to work and say, "I don't want to fight. I want peace. I don't want to disturb my peace." And this peace is the main thing. If you have peace then you know the art of love. If you have no peace, then where is the love? Peace is needed first to love. Otherwise love will become only words. And words are not love. Words will never cook rice. This is my last thing to you. God bless you. ❧

The Lightness of Being

The blink of an eye
The snap of a finger
When it ends, we are surprised
Even though we knew it was coming all along.
Is it a dream?
Is it a game?
Is it a test?
What is it?
When it is over, they say we are gone
But what is the truth?
We are gone, but still here
Like the tree that drops its leaves
It looks as if it is dead
But it returns again and again.
We can learn from nature
Because we are nature.
The form is different
But the function is the same.
The end is the start
Of a new beginning.
The line becomes a circle.
Let us rejoice
In this fleeting moment of time.

Back to India

THE day I left India after my first visit, a thought came into my mind: *I want to travel around the world*. The three-month trip to India at the age of forty-one to study Yoga had ignited a long-dormant travel bug. While in India, besides the diarrhea, I caught a full-blown case of the travel virus. Shortly after I got back to my job as a school counselor in Minneapolis, I put in a request for a full year of leave without pay for the next school year. I know my principal thought I was crazy, but fortunately she liked me enough to grant the leave. She could tell I wanted it very much and would leave anyway, one way or another. My mind was made up. I was approved to take a full year off. It was an exciting time. I planned out a travel agenda.

The first leg of my travels turned out to be a six-week return journey to India with Swami Hari. We had met on the previous trip and spent a lot of time together. He came to the US for the first time shortly after I returned from that previous trip. When I left India on that day in February of 1999 I never dreamed I would see him again. When I greeted him in Minneapolis in May of 1999, I immediately told him, without thinking, that I was going back to India with him. It turned out to be a good thing. He was sick on that return trip and needed someone to assist him through the airport, carrying the luggage and checking details. I describe Swami Hari's visits to the US in more detail in *Swami Hari: I am a simple forest monk*.

Our return trip to India was scheduled for September of

1999. Swami Hari had about $10,000 in donations people had given him after his talks during the past summer. He traveled to various Yoga centers in the US and talked about his life as a monk in the Himalayas. He spent many years in isolation doing intense meditative practices in the holy Shiva shrine of Tarkeshwar. On one of his outings, while traveling in California, someone said they would donate a dozen computers to him. He came back to Minneapolis from that trip with the idea of starting a computer school in the remote Himalayan mountain village of Toli (eventually the school moved to Malethi and was renamed SRIVERM). I thought it sounded like a crazy idea, but he was set on it. There was no electricity in Toli, and I thought: How can you run a computer school on generators? He was adamant that the money would be used for the school. He gave me the cash to carry back. He was worried what customs would think if he were carrying $10,000 out of the US.

We were brought to the airport in Minneapolis by some friends and went to wait in the ticket line. We thought he was supposed to have an e-ticket, so when we were helping him pack we never were concerned about the location of the ticket. It turned out it was not an e-ticket, and it was missing. We tried calling his travel agent, but it was Sunday and the office was closed. We tried talking to the manager of the airline ticket counter, but to no avail. We searched all the suitcases, compartments, and folders. We called back to The Meditation Center where he had stayed and asked them to look around. They could not find it. Time was passing and the flight departure was less than an hour away. For an international flight, that was cutting it close. We inquired what a one-way ticket would cost if we bought it right then, and it was $7000. I felt the money in my pocket and knew we could afford to buy a ticket, but his dream of a computer school would be finished. While he and a couple of friends were at the counter trying to decide what to do, I went back for one more search of his suitcase. I thought we had checked everywhere, but I looked again inside one of the more hidden pockets, then inside a folder. I found it, to a great sense of relief, mixed in between a bunch of papers. We were on our way.

I put the $10,000 into one of the pockets of my lightweight cargo pants. I was a professional traveler by that time. I cut my hair very short, packed lightly, and had state-of-the-art quick-drying clothes. Even the attendant taking tickets commented to me, "There's a guy who knows how to travel." Swami Hari was ill, and the flight attendant noticed something was wrong. He was seated in the first class section since the person who sponsored his trip had wanted him to travel in comfort. The flight attendant was concerned about him and she saw that I was escorting him. Rather than go back to the economy class, she invited me to sit in the empty seat beside him so I could help keep an eye on him. What a great way to travel on a long trip. The seats lean back fully making it much easier to get some rest and lessen the jet lag. I was enjoying this travel experience.

Swami Hari sat upright in his seat the whole way, meditating, with his wool cap pulled down over his eyes. On the leg to Amsterdam, there was a cattle rancher from Oklahoma sitting near him. He could see I was traveling with him and was very curious. He asked me some questions about him. I told him he was a vegetarian from birth and had renounced the world quite a few years ago when he became a swami. This cattle rancher had never heard of such a thing and could not believe someone could live as a vegetarian. I told him that Swami Hari was meditating during the flight, and this caused an even greater curiosity in him.

He asked, "You mean he just sits there the whole time doing nothing?"

I answered, "Something like that, but not quite. When someone meditates, the mind is still focused on something, so it is different than daydreaming."

It went on like that for a few minutes until I went back

to resting. After we landed we never saw the rancher again. Perhaps if the man spent more time with Swami Hari he would have become a student of his.

We stayed in Delhi with some friends that first night back in India. The next day before heading north to Rishikesh, he assigned someone to take me on a tour of the city. As we were walking through various markets and tourist spots, I became acutely aware of the $10,000 in cash sitting in my pocket. Someone had told me that Delhi was the pickpocket capital of the world and that I should be very careful. I was very concerned and constantly had a hand on my pocket to make sure the money was still there. It turned out OK, but I was happy to get out of there and on to the next leg of the journey.

We stopped in Rishikesh for a couple of days, but I spent most of that trip in Tarkeshwar, where Swami Hari had spent so many years. Tarkeshwar is mentioned in *Living with the Himalayan Masters* by Swami Rama. It is a spiritually charged place. Swami Hari was grateful for all the help I had given him on his stay in the US, so he invited me there as his guest. I went to Tarkeshwar a couple of days before Swami Hari because he had some other business to attend to regarding the computer school.

The ride to Tarkeshwar was interesting, to say the least. Something I ate the night before had left me with a case of moderate diarrhea, or so I thought. The second I got in the taxi for the six-hour ride, the diarrhea became worse. It continued to get much worse over the next couple of hours. We stopped in the last large village on the way to pick up some fresh vegetables and I ran out of the taxi to try and find a bathroom. A white Minnesotan like me really sticks out and a crowd started gathering around our taxi to have a look at me. I had experienced this before and was kind of used to it. But I had more on my mind than the large crowd. I needed to find a toilet, and fast. I looked around quickly, but there was none in sight. The longer I walked and searched for a bathroom, the bigger the crowd grew. I was walking quickly and the people were curious as to where I was going, but I still could not find a toilet. Finally, I saw a place where the pigs were wallowing in the garbage. I walked into the middle of that mess, pulled down my pants and squatted. The people who were watching me dispersed after they saw what I was doing. I made my way back to the taxi. I had to ask the driver to stop quickly several more times along the way while I ran into the forest to relieve myself.

In addition to all those bathroom stops, the ride to Tarkeshwar became even stranger. On the steepest, narrowest, and most winding mountain road of the trip, it started pouring rain. It was raining so hard that we couldn't even see out the windows of the taxi. To add to the dilemma, the windshield wipers in the cab were not working. The driver had to lean out the window to see the road. How he was able to navigate the road without going over the side was a mystery to me. We arrived safely, but what a harrowing adventure it turned out to be. I was put through quite a test to have the opportunity and privilege to visit Tarkeshwar.

A couple of days after I arrived in Tarkeshwar, Swami Hari joined me there. It was his first time back after his US trip. The reunion of Swami Hari and Tarkeshwar was such a joyful thing to watch. There is a walk of several hundred yards from the taxi drop off to the ashram. I watched him very carefully. He walked slowly with such a full awareness. It was as if he was taking in everything, like a wine connoisseur would take in a high quality wine. He was becoming part of nature again. It is a remote forest area at an elevation of about 6,500 feet, with large deodar fir trees and wild animals such as mountain lions, tigers, and bears. He was not the Wizard of Oz, but it has the feel of an enchanted forest. He was becoming one with nature, in the way he had been for those fifteen years he had lived there in almost complete isolation. He got into a trance-like state. That first night back they made a campfire, and Swami Hari was chant-

ing in Sanskrit. It was the most joyous chanting I have ever
heard, before or since. He was so grateful and happy to be
back after his first world-travel experience.

I stayed in Tarkeshwar for twenty-six nights, but after
only a few days my meditation battery was charged with
intense spiritual energy and I had to ease up on the Meditation practice. I had reached full capacity, and anything
beyond that was more than my system was ready to take
in. Just like a rechargeable battery plugged in too long, my
nervous system could get damaged from the strong flow of
energy. So for the rest of my stay I combined the daily Meditation practice with a lot of walking on the mountain trails.
The views were spectacular. From certain spots I could see
the snow capped ranges of the Himalayas.

Most goods and services travel by donkey from village to
village, so there are plenty of hiking paths. You just have to
follow the donkey trails. Shortly after my arrival in Tarkeshwar, I was bathing in a mountain creek by the ashram.
There was no running water or electricity in the ashram,
so the only other option for bathing was a bucket shower.
I liked bathing in the creek better than the bucket option. I
thought I was out of the way and concealed, so I took off all
my clothes, squatted in the creek, and started cleaning myself. A few minutes into the bath I heard the familiar sound
of the donkey line coming. They wear bells in case they get
lost or move off the trail. The owner can then find them by
listening for the bells. It turned out I was right in the middle of a donkey trail and they walked right past me as I was
squatting there. The people leading the donkeys gave me
a funny look but did not say anything. The next day, however, I had a new nickname around the area. They started to
call me Naga Baba. It is a type of swami who has renounced
everything, even the clothes they wear. They walk around
nude all the time, even in the harshest of weather conditions. They do not even use blankets when they sleep in the
winter. They see the body as a blanket for the soul. Of course

I was no Naga Baba and the people were only teasing when they called me that.

The only time I left the Tarkeshwar Valley during my stay was for the inauguration of the first computer school that Swami Hari had started. He planned the groundbreaking on October 26, the same day as Swami Rama's birthday. Swami Rama was his "Master" in the spiritual sense. The party was in Toli, the home village of both Swami Hari and Swami Rama. So it was a duel celebration: the birthday and the inauguration. At that time, it was a three- or four-hour hike through the mountains to get to Toli. There were hundreds of villagers from all the surrounding areas. I was the only white guy around that area for who knows how many miles. Normally I am color blind to such things, but I noticed it quite clearly as I looked around the crowd, and I am sure they noticed me. Swami Hari introduced me to the crowd during his speech and they treated me like a special guest. My picture and an article made the local newspapers.

After the ceremony we left to have lunch in the Swami Rama family home. An Indian man who I had met recently at the Ashram kept rushing me to finish and I couldn't figure out why. He wanted me to come outside with him. So I finished up my lunch and went with him. Swami Hari was sitting outside on the veranda. This man went up to Swami Hari with a cup of water, and then lay prone on the ground in front of him. Swami Hari took off his shawl, placed it over the man, said a few blessings, and sprinkled water on him. I had just witnessed a most unusual initiation ceremony. That man had just renounced and become a swami. Swami Hari gave him the name of Swami Hari Bundu, or brother of Swami Hari. The next day I went into the local village barber with the man, and he had his head shaved. That is the custom for a renunciation ceremony like that, but usually it is done beforehand. This was a spontaneous event. People said it was an auspicious time and place for a ceremony like that.

I returned to Tarkeshwar for several more days, and at the end of my twenty-six night stay I got a ride back to Rishikesh with some other visitors who were returning to town. When I arrived at Tarkeshwar I did not know when I would find a ride back or how long I would stay. Unlike the arrival ride, the return ride was very uneventful. In Gematria, or Hebrew numerology, 26 is the number that represents the holiest name of God. So staying there twenty-six nights was very meaningful to me. I stayed a few more days in Rishikesh before it was time to move on. I said goodbye to Swami Hari and all my new friends and got a taxi back to Delhi for the plane ride home.

It Started with a Whisper

A look inside
Through the peephole
We see our reflection
If only briefly
A peak at the Divine?
Who am I?
A winding road
A fresh breeze
A flame rekindles
A gentle nudge
A change of heart
Which seems so small
Changes the world
The choices we make
Reveal our destiny
The future disappears
As the moment arrives

Teaching Yoga?

I am not a Yoga teacher, but I have "taught" Yoga since 1995. If someone invites me to give a class, I sit in the front and open my mouth. If something comes out, then I talk. If someone hears it, that is great. If someone learns something, that is better. But I am definitely not a teacher. All I am doing is passing on what someone taught me. As my teachers have clearly shown me, to be fully effective, a Yoga teacher needs to tap into the ancient flow of knowledge and be well grounded in their own practice. A student needs to self-monitor so eventually he or she can rely on the "teacher within," and not be dependent on an outside teacher. An outside teacher is more like a trigger, or guide. They should be shown the proper respect, but not idolized in any way. A student needs to be careful of being dependent on a teacher. If a teacher notices a student in any way becoming dependent, this needs to be discouraged immediately.

The "I am not a Yoga teacher" philosophy can be quite confusing to people. For example, one time I arrived to give a class and someone asked me if I was teaching the class tonight. I replied with a simple no.

The person who asked me panicked and said, "If you are not teaching the class, who is?"

She ran and checked the schedule and said that my name was penciled in, so why wasn't I teaching the class. I told her, "I don't teach. But if you'd like me to enter the classroom and sit in the front and see what happens, I would be fine with that."

She smiled and said, "You can be so difficult sometimes."

Another time a woman walked into the Yoga classroom on the first night of class. I was sitting in front of the room in the usual place that the teacher would sit.

"Are you the teacher?" she asked.

I told her no and she went to sit down. I began to speak and led the class for the next two hours.

She came to me after the class and said, "You said you were not the teacher. Will we have a different person leading the class next week?"

I replied, "I plan to be here."

"But you are not the teacher?" she asked.

"No," I answered. I am sure she was confused and thought I was really weird. She continued with the four-week class and didn't mention it again. I ran into her a couple of years later after she had completed a Yoga teacher training course. She told me she remembered what I had said to her that first class and she finally understand what I meant. We both laughed about it.

At first, when I was asked to go into a Yoga teacher training program after about a year of study, I said yes. It was a way to continue taking classes. It was fun and I learned a lot. I already had a regular practice at home and it was a way to continue to deepen the practice in a supportive environment. When it came time to do my student teaching, I was much more resistant. I was a licensed teacher in the Minneapolis Public Schools, but this was a whole different thing. To teach Yoga and Meditation in this style was beyond what I could see myself doing. It is a gentle Hatha Yoga from the ancient Himalayan Tradition. It goes well beyond simply doing postures and pushing yourself into all sorts of strange positions. It emphasizes guided relaxation and breathing, with a slower, contemplative pace to the postures. On top of that, it is all combined with awareness of a mantra. I had all sorts of doubts. How could I teach relaxation if I wasn't relaxed myself? Even if I could get relaxed at home, how could I reach a state like that in front of a class?

Finally, after some months of prodding by several people, I did my student teaching. It was challenging. I didn't know all the techniques and the best way to teach them. I read and re-read the Yoga books to memorize the suggested steps to learn a particular posture. It took a long time to feel comfortable. I took classes from as many different Yoga teachers as I could and continued to study. Over time I was able to formulate an idea of what I liked in a Yoga teacher. Finally, I found one or two teachers who taught Yoga in the way that I imagined it should be taught. I used what I learned from them to continue to develop a style that fit me and felt like the right way of doing it. Eventually I developed a teaching style that I enjoyed and that felt effective. But I still didn't call myself a teacher. It is a lifelong learning process where the feeling of being a student never ends.

I also continued a regular practice at home. Having a regular practice and learning from personal experience is the best way to learn to teach. I had such a struggle in learning Yoga that I could easily identify with students who had all sorts of physical and emotional ailments. I started out with a very stiff and achy body that was recovering from many injuries. I also had a mind that was hyper and had a lot of difficulty in focusing when it came to practicing Meditation. It took me many months to do a pain-free forward bend and to sit still on a meditation cushion for more than a few minutes. After twenty years my body and mind have changed a lot, but I remember the struggles along the way. Of course I still have a long way to go, but it is rewarding to see the progress. There is always something to challenge us in Yoga. It is a continuum. There is no such thing as advanced or beginning. We all start from wherever we are and go to wherever we can. If someone is born with the ability to twist themselves into all sorts of positions and is very limber, are they advanced? No, they begin where they are and progress, or not, from that point.

For that reason, it is important that students do not look at other students in the class and compare themselves to them. This is not helpful and can lead to negative emotions like envy and sadness. Here is an example from my experience in a school setting. If a student starts out scoring 5 percent on a standardized test and progresses to scoring 50 percent by the end of the year, that is tremendous progress. But in a standardized system, they are still considered to be failing and have not mastered the material. The teacher and student did a phenomenal job, but if an outsider looks at the test scores, they will see a failing student, and not notice the great teacher. It doesn't take into account the most important statistic: the amount of growth exhibited by the student. That is what really matters.

To be called a teacher, someone who is listening to the class has to learn something. If someone is standing in front of a group and talking, does this mean they are teaching? The answer is clearly no. It doesn't matter how many degrees someone has, how many years they have practiced, who their teachers were, or how highly they think of themselves. What matters is the relationship between the teacher and the student at that moment in time. If learning is taking place, who is teaching and who is learning? Where does the teaching come from? We have so many choices to make as a teacher. What we choose to say or do at any particular moment in time has to be inspired. It is all about the intention behind what someone says, and not necessarily the words that come out. It has to flow through us from a source larger than ourselves. This is how people learn what they need to learn at the time they need to learn it. Teachers become conduits, opening to an ancient flow of energy and information. If you meet a teacher who thinks they personally are the source, they are probably exhausted from being a round-the-clock caregiver to such a huge ego. I have a theory about teaching Yoga: The students who come to the class are actually the teachers. When I am sitting in front of a class, I thank all the students for coming to help me. A group of students focusing their attention on a teacher all at the same time can create a very powerful energy force. The energy can go back and forth and everybody present can benefit, not only the "students."

Practicing Yoga in a meditative way is much more than simply going through a series of poses and twisting your body into funny positions. It is a process of observing the inner dialogue. We study that dialogue and learn patterns and habits of the mind. We learn that most thoughts that distract us are either worries about past actions or anxieties about future actions. They are only thoughts and they have no life to them other than what we give them. When we relieve ourselves of the burden of the past and future, we are left with the present. If we are in the present, have pure and loving intentions, and practice regularly, then we allow ourselves to be open to the flow. We can access the "teacher within" and learn to ride the wave of eternal wisdom. May the flow be with you. ≈

To Be Alive

Be aware
Feel the flow
Understand the moment
Take it in
Be totally here
Discover
What it means
To
Be Alive

The Tunnel Inside

I recently completed my five-year colonoscopy follow-up and got a great tour of the tunnel inside of me. In case you are not familiar with a colonoscopy, it is Western medicine's version of the Complete Wash we do in Yoga. Before the procedure could be done, a thorough cleansing of my large intestine (or colon) had to be completed. At the start of the procedure, a physician trained in endoscopy inserted a lubricated scope in my anus. The doctor then gently guided the scope through my colon. The images of the magnified, well-lit tunnel were projected on a large screen TV. If you haven't had the pleasure yet of this experience, it is like seeing your own private Discovery Channel TV show. This was my second colonoscopy. I had my first one at age fifty, and because at that time they found a polyp, even though it was benign, they highly recommended a five-year follow-up. That is how I ended up doing another colonoscopy at age fifty-five. Each stage of it went well and this time the doctor did not find any polyps or other problems.

Since this was my second time, every step of the process was familiar and I was much more comfortable with the whole thing. They have a new "lower volume" cleansing solution and offered me the choice of using that or the one where you drink a gallon of water. I chose the lower volume method, and it worked well. Just like the saline-induced Yoga Complete Wash, the object is for the bowel movement to become a clear liquid. That is how you know you have completed a successful cleansing (and Complete Wash).

The doctor complemented me several times as he was moving the scope through the colon on my great prep job. I have found that one of the keys to this is eating lightly for a couple of days before. It is the same type of preparation you would do for the Yoga Complete Wash, so if you have experience with that, it is very helpful.

I was awake to hear the doctor's compliments and talked to him and the nurse during the procedure. Like the first time I had the procedure five years ago, I declined any sedation. This allowed me to remain fully conscious the whole time. We discussed what the doctor was seeing along the way. The whole tour took less than thirty minutes. Normally they don't let outside observers come into the room and watch the procedure. The designated driver has to wait in the lobby, and that is what my wife Nikki had to do when she drove me five years ago. But after that first procedure I was so enthusiastic and thrilled with what I had seen that this time Nikki wanted to watch it. So I called the doctor's office ahead of time and got approval from the doctor for Nikki to observe the procedure. When the nurse called my name, she followed me into the back area and sat quietly in the corner of the examination room.

The doctor was like a tour guide leading a sightseeing expedition. He gave us a detailed narrative of what we were watching on the TV screen. The various sections of the large colon add up to about five feet long (one and a half meters). The large intestine is smooth with ridges, and you see the light-colored blood vessels against the whitish-pink background all along the way. The doctor could see that both Nikki and I were enjoying his detailed description so he went one step further than usual. When he reached the point where the large intestine ends (cecum) and the small intestine begins (ileum) he moved the probe through the flap-like valve opening into the small intestine. This peek was enlightening. The small intestine looked like an exotic fish at the bottom of the ocean with its bristling, soft, brushlike projections that are called villi. Wow! That view alone was worth the price of admission.

I don't know yet if I will decide to have another colonoscopy five or ten years down the road and I have some time to think about it. But I am glad I tried it these two times, and am elated for my clean bill of health. It is a very satisfying feeling to empty your colon. It brightened my mood, energized me, and cleared my mind during my morning Meditation. I already have a plan to do the Complete Wash (minus the colonoscopy) next spring. I am looking forward to the emotional, spiritual, and health benefits it brings. ❧

It's Not Mine

What changes in the winds of time, space, and energy

Cause a human birth

There is no beginning or end

It is only a circle

Each birth forever changes the course of history

To Be Born

EVERYONE loves babies. They turn the edgiest person into the softest mush. They bring out the instincts to care for and protect in all of us. Recently I met a baby who was only a few days old named Somayaaga. Spending a little time with him allowed me to see a glimpse of the world from his perspective. He came into the world with seemingly no knowledge at all, but he instantly became my teacher. He reminded me that to be born means you start over again. Every single thing has to be learned about the world. It is all new. Someone has to feed you, bathe you, change your diaper, treat any health problems, and basically take care of your every need. Someone needs to teach you all the basic skills and knowledge that allow you to operate in the world.

I don't have the answers about why I was born, but I do know that in the fifty-five years I have been on the planet I have become attached to being in the body and all that comes with it. The smells, sights, sounds, food, people, email, computers, TV, walking, sleeping, and on and on are all things to which I have grown accustomed. The attachments are countless. I am attached to so many things that have taken many years to become a part of me, that I am not even aware of everything that I am attached to. As we learn how to operate in the world, all these attachments become second nature to us and we are no longer conscious of all of them. The planet feels like it has become my home, and the only home I remember. An even greater mystery for me now more than birth is the mystery of death. They are very connected to each other and hard to separate. They are locked together as partners in the life cycle. It is a contract for all of us: with birth comes death. Eventually everyone who comes into a body has to leave it behind. We have proof of that. But clearly I am having a lot of trouble understanding the reality of my own eventual death.

The idea that someday I will shrivel up, disappear, and my memory will be erased is so difficult for me to fully comprehend and come to terms with. Occasionally the idea of it wakes me up in the middle of the night, sometimes with sweats and a rapid heart rate. This issue is ongoing for me, and at times, very pressing in my mind. It does not totally consume me because most of the time I go about my life and forget about it. But then some thought or event triggers it and reminds me of it all over again. I can say that it is the driving force behind my life, and I am especially reminded of it when I sit down to meditate. It drives me to my Meditation practice, and it keeps me striving for purpose in my life at every turn. The idea of not wanting to lose my consciousness at death is an incredibly strong force within me. I am still trying to figure out what I can best do with my time now so I can be prepared for the eventual time of leaving the body and this world behind. When I leave I want the attachments to be done, so that I am leaving it all behind without a second thought. I can practice for this, but I will not know until the time comes how prepared I actually am.

Even if we are reborn, the question remains if we carry any memories with us. Some people, including great spiritual masters such as Swami Rama, have said this is possible. But all I know is my personal experience, and I can't remember anything about a possible past life. Somewhere along the way from death to birth I lost these memories. Perhaps it is at the moment we leave our body behind and our brain ceases to function that our memories completely disappear. There is nothing to store them in anymore. But, is it possible that we carry something forward and that some momentum or deep consciousness comes with us? I know that various religions and Yoga philosophies have a precise belief in what it is we carry forward, but it is difficult for me to accept these ideas unconditionally as the truth. I have not yet come to a personal belief or understanding of this process. I think this belief can only be gained by personal experience, but once we have shed the body, we have also lost our ability to speak or write about it.

The cycle of birth to death to rebirth is commonly believed to occur in some form in many religious and spiritual beliefs. These beliefs may have begun through observing the natural agricultural cycles that mimic this process. From my understanding, Hindu philosophy states that all people born on this earth are certain to die, and equally certain to be reborn after death. It is believed that we are born with Samskaras, or a kind of spiritual imprint from the previous life. Similar to Hinduism, in Buddhism death is not seen as the end of life, it is merely the end of the body we inhabit in this life. Our spirit will still remain and seek out, through the need for attachment, a new body and new life. Many of the religions and spiritual philosophies emphasize the impermanence of life and all that we cherish and hold on to.

It is clear to me, thanks to Somayaaga's reminder, that when we are reborn we lose our memory of how to function in the human body. The brain of a newborn is not developed enough to carry all that skill and knowledge. At death we leave our body behind. That is also clear to me because of the physical proof. It is unclear to me how or if it is possible to carry some memories forward with no physical body to store it in. No wonder there is such a fear of death. It seems like everything we know and have learned will be wiped out. It all has to be re-learned if and when we are reborn. It is a daunting thought. We have to learn the language and the skills of whatever time period, location, and species we arrive in. We are completely dependent on whoever is raising us to teach us. Dying is truly the greatest act of renunciation. And it is something everyone does. I don't know where, when, or if the answers will come to me about death. Perhaps they will only come when I encounter it directly at that precise point in time.

Somayaaga also reminded me of all the devotion it took for my parents to raise me. How do we ever thank our parents for all the love they showed us as babies? My memories were erased from any previous life, and they were also erased from when I was a baby. When we are old enough and conscious enough to see another baby and realize how much constant love and care it takes to raise one, it shows us how much we ourselves were cared for. I am just now starting to understand the love my parents showed for me. It is now over twenty years since my parents passed away. With this new realization how can I ever thank them? One way I can think of to thank them is to learn to enjoy life and make the most of this opportunity.

There are all sorts of stories about people who learn they are dying soon due to an illness and come to appreciate life more than they ever had. They start to come into the moment and realize each day is a new opportunity. What can we learn from all of this? We go through a lot during the process of being born. You have to learn how to operate your body and mind all over again and make many mistakes along the way. After all that work, we need to rejoice in every second of life knowing we took a leap of faith, willingly or not, and it worked out. That leap of faith has allowed us to be alive and witness all the wonders and drama that this life has to offer. To show a gratitude for this and to make all of it worthwhile, we need to have fun while in the body and enjoy life each and every moment. Of course, this is easier said than done, and the skill of enjoying life remains an ongoing challenge for me. But if we can master this challenge, it is surely one way to thank the people who brought us into the world.

The last time I saw Somayaaga before finishing this essay was at the Guru Purnima celebration in Minneapolis with

Swami Veda on July 3, 2012. He was now three and a half months old. I held him on my lap for a few minutes before the ceremony started. Afterward, while sitting in the group meditation, a thought flashed in my mind. This was Somayaaga's first Guru Purnima, and he could live to celebrate it for the next hundred years. That would bring his life to the year 2112, long after I have left this body. I don't have the vision or imagination to know what changes he will see in his life over the next hundred years, but whatever happens in his lifetime, at least I have been a small part of it. ✤

NOTE: *Somayaaga was born to Aaron and Saras on March 19, 2012.*

The Spaceship

The spaceship
Traveling on the planet earth
With the most advanced technology
Ever developed
On automatic pilot
Until someday
Something comes along to
Force us into a new
Flight pattern
Manual pilot must be used
As if we are a born again baby
Learning to crawl and walk
Before we can run
And eventually fly again
This time higher
More on the edge
Guided by the radar
Of love and harmony

Biofeedback and Beyond

BIOFEEDBACK has deep roots in the Himalayan Tradition of Yoga Meditation. Swami Rama, founder of this worldwide Tradition, is considered one of the pioneers of modern-day biofeedback. In experiments done at the Menninger Foundation in Topeka, Kansas, in 1970, **Swami Rama astonished scientists with his ability to regulate what was previously thought of as the "involuntary" autonomic nervous system functions.** The experiments he participated in are well documented and explained in depth in the book *Beyond Biofeedback* by Elmer & Alyce Green.

Under laboratory conditions he demonstrated the following:

1. He increased the temperature difference between the left and right side of one hand to 11 degrees Fahrenheit. This caused the left side of his hand to become pink and the right side to become gray. Dr. Green described this demonstration as "showing exquisite differential control over this normally uncontrolled piece of the neural apparatus."
2. He stopped his heart from pumping blood for 16.2 seconds while sitting motionless during the demonstration.

He returned to the Menninger Foundation several months later and did other brain wave and psychokinetic experiments that are also documented in *Beyond Biofeedback*.

Today biofeedback has all sorts of medical applications. It is considered efficacious for anxiety, attention deficit disorder, headache (adult), hypertension, temporomandibular disorders and urinary incontinence. It is considered probably efficacious for many other disorders including alcoholism and substance abuse and chronic pain.

I first got interested in biofeedback after being diagnosed with a hyperthyroid condition in 1999. I had already been studying Yoga and Meditation for several years, so I was very interested to experiment with the various relaxation and breathing exercises I had learned to see which one would be most helpful. I bought a heart rate monitor watch, which is commonly used by runners. This is a biofeedback instrument because it gives constant information on a biological sign—the heart rate. I found that two-to-one breathing, where the exhalation is doubled, was the most helpful for me. This is because the exhalation is associated with the parasympathetic side of the autonomic nervous system. By extending the exhalation, the heart rate slows down.

I continued to use biofeedback to supplement other medical treatments I received for my thyroid condition. I believe that this practice allowed me to take less allopathic medicine. Eventually, due to an herbal extract remedy called bugleweed, I was able to get off the allopathic medicine entirely. After a year or two of taking the bugleweed, my blood tests moved into normal range, so I was able to stop taking it as well. Of course the results vary from person to person and should always be done under the guidance of a physician.

My interest remained high, so after a few years of informal practice, I decided to formalize my study of biofeedback. I invested in some expensive equipment, and after about a year of training, practice, and being mentored, I became a Certified Biofeedback Practitioner. I practice the Relaxation Model of Biofeedback, which uses the same relaxation and breathing techniques as taught in the Himalayan Yoga Tradition. Detailed information on what it takes to become certified can be found at the Biofeedback Certification International Alliance website, www.bcia.org.

Two pieces of biofeedback equipment that are reasonable to buy and effective for practice at home are the previously mentioned heart rate monitor and the thermistor. The thermistor measures changes in skin temperature through a sensor that you tape to your finger. As a person relaxes, the skin temperature rises. The list of biofeedback devices that you can purchase for a reasonable price and use at home is growing. This is due to all the iPhone and iPad applications that are now available.

Through personal practice and working with many clients over the last few years. I have found that there are three keys to learning self regulation:

1. Correct diaphragmatic breathing.
2. Rate of breathing (five to seven cycles per minute most quickly balances the nervous system). More information can be found on this if you look up *Resonant Frequency Breathing* on Google.
3. Nurturing positive emotions in the Heart Center such as love, gratitude, and joy.

Learning self-regulation through biofeedback is very similar to learning how to meditate. One similarity is that you "allow" yourself to relax rather than "try" to do it. Biofeedback supports a quantitative approach to this process. I have found this approach to be very helpful over the years for myself and clients I have worked with. For more information, see the "Biofeedback" page at www.themeditation center.org.

The Knock on the Door

What is this fleeting thing
Called life
Here now and
Gone the next
When are words
The last words
Never known
Until the time arrives
We are always surprised
But somewhere
Deep inside
We know all along
Like a long-lost memory
Dwelling below the surface
Waiting until
The knock on the door

Time Marches On

IT is relentless. The march of time does not stop for any-one. But how do we really know time is moving on? We can look at the clock and the calendar, but somehow I don't quite trust it. There is something artificial or human-made about it. I am still trying to figure out why there are sixty minutes in an hour and sixty seconds in a minute. Why couldn't each hour be ninety minutes, and then we would only have sixteen hours in a day? The current year on the Ethiopian calendar is 2005, not 2013. In the Hebrew calendar the year is 5773. Using a clock or calendar is not quite as clear as it seems at first glance.

We can look at the human-made objects around us and see that over time they need repair and replacement, but there is also something artificial about that. Material objects wear out at different rates. Everything will eventually deteriorate, but the rates are so different, that it is an inconsistent way to measure time. Our own body is obviously an indicator that time is marching on. But at certain stages of life that can happen at such a slow rate that we don't notice the changes. When we look in the mirror every day it is nearly impossible to notice the changes. Furthermore, everyone ages at a different rate, so this is also a very inconsistent method. Nevertheless, if we compare pictures of ourselves taken several years apart, we can obviously see the changes.

I always thought the change of seasons was the best measure of time, but then I lived in Panama for a year, which is near the equator. Daytime and nighttime hours are almost equal year-round. The temperature has little or no change from day to night and season to season. I know time passed while we were there because a year on the calendar went by, but simply going by the changes in the seasons did not work in Panama. Sometimes I dream of bringing some of our Panamanian friends up here to experience the winter season. It would be interesting to get their reaction. Snow has never, ever fallen in Panama City, and I would love to see the looks on their faces during one of the Minnesota blizzards.

After returning to live in Minnesota in June of 2009 after the year in Panama, I was finally able to witness this onslaught of the march of time again. It was the changing of the seasons that did it. But when I first came back, I did not believe the seasons would change. Sometimes it seemed as if summer would go on forever. And why not? That's what happened in Panama. How could those long daylight hours not go on forever? How could the warm summer breezes ever leave us behind? Lounging in the lawn chair on our patio, I actually began to believe that it would not happen. I honestly thought that perhaps for the first time in our known history, winter would not come. Why not, I thought. We live in an unpredictable world, so why should the changing of the seasons be so predictable. Why couldn't summer go on forever? Maybe the climate had changed so much in my year in Panama that even winter would leave us behind.

I began to really doubt that the season would change. Show me, I thought. Let me be a witness to the change and then I can believe once more. Soon after, as the summer breezes started to cool, nature responded to my doubts. As I looked out the window one morning there was frost on the roof of the garage. I could easily notice that the daylight became shorter. Eventually I could not sit and read on the back patio any longer. It was too cold for that. I started to believe that it was getting colder, but I was still not convinced that it would change all the way to winter. And for a while it looked like I was right. November of 2009 turned out to be much warmer than average. It turned out to be the second warmest November in 118 years of record keeping. For the first time ever in my life, I could comfortably ride my bicycle outdoors for the whole month of November. I thought, "Aha!" I was right all along, there is not going to be a winter. But by mid-December the high temperature each day was less than 32 degrees F and by the end of December there was two feet of snow on the ground. Hallelujah, I was a believer once again!

The changing of the seasons is an incredible thing to behold. Nature seems so unstable, but in the end, maybe it is the most stable thing that we have. Sure as time itself, it happens. It is such a thing to witness. In an unpredictable world, the changing of the seasons is so predictable. How could this be, I marveled. I had somehow forgotten what the change in seasons was really like and what it really meant. But once again, nature followed the familiar path and showed me the way.

7 Billion

7 billion people
All sailing
On the same ship
What fuel drives the engine
What wind blows the sails
Some jump ship
But most stay until
They are forced to leave
Many depart each day
Many arrive
Living together as
A family
Locked into an
Unknown destiny
Humanity the common bond

Why Collect Things?

CHANCES are that one day humans will not be roaming this planet. In his book *The World Without Us*, Alan Weisman writes, "Humans are going extinct eventually. Everything has so far. It's like death: there's no reason to think we're any different." Once humans leave, all the other items associated with humanity will eventually deteriorate. This means that the libraries, the internet, the clothes in our closets, and the money in our pockets will all disappear over time. But long before that day comes, as we pass on because of old age or illness, all our items will be left behind. That is a fact about which we can be certain. When we die, we bring nothing with us.

Several years ago my wife and I were in the process of moving to Panama for a year because of a job opportunity for Nikki. We rented out our house, and the person renting it wanted it completely emptied of all our possessions. We don't consider ourselves materialists who buy and save a lot of things. Even so, we threw out or gave away literally a hundred bags of unneeded items. That started me thinking about all the things people collect. Things just seem to pile up if you have the room and stay in one place long enough. Everything that comes into a house that is not eaten has to be removed by someone. It is amazing what the two of us had collected while living in a small house for less than four years.

Everyone has a different way of sorting through their stuff. My wife Nikki takes her time and is very thoughtful.

I like to go through my things quickly and not ponder too long on whether to keep something or not, but I still get stuck now and then on what to do with certain things. After a while it wears me down and I lose my patience, and then it gets easier to start throwing things out or giving them away. Even then, though, when I unearth some endearing and sentimental things, it is very wrenching trying to figure out what to do. Is there really a need for me to keep a trophy I won in fifth grade for Little League baseball? At the time it was thrilling, but what is the purpose now? And what about all those yearbooks collected from seventh to twelfth grade? If I haven't looked at them for thirty years, what are the chances I will use them in the future? The list goes on, but in the end I either need to get rid of those things or the person who cleans up my mess after I leave the planet has to get rid of them. Why put someone through all that when it is something I could have done long before?

Both my parents are deceased, and I inherited a lot of "things" from them. Eventually, I went through everything and kept only what I considered to be the most meaningful pictures and documents. I distilled it down to one small box for each of them. This process inspired me to do the same with my "things." I decided to get all of my most treasured personal items down to one box. It was not easy. It was quite an inward-looking exercise. It caused me to really look at my life in the big picture and ask myself this question: If I only had one box to share with the world after I was gone, what would I put in it? That box is now stored in a closet with a label on the top that says, "Highlights in the Life of Daniel Hertz." I have no idea what will eventually happen to it, but going through that process was definitely worthwhile for my peace of mind. By doing this now I am saving someone else the trouble of doing it later on.

But what will happen to the items in that box? If Nikki or a relative or friend keeps something from the box, eventually they will also be gone and then what happens? Even if it gets passed on to someone else, how long will that last? Maybe until the end of that person's life, then it will probably get thrown out. We have no children, and even if we had, what would they do with it? At best they would keep it on a shelf somewhere and look through it every ten or fifteen years or whenever they had to move themselves. Eventually, after one generation or two, it would be thrown out, lost, forgotten, or simply deteriorate. Traveling through life with a lighter burden of goods feels better, like I am doing the right thing for the people left behind. ✺

The Stranger

Another human
Living on the planet

A person
We have not met

Perhaps someone
Not born yet

Someday this stranger
Could save our life

Someday this stranger
Could be our best friend

Someday this stranger
Could be our spouse

Someday this stranger
Could marry our child

Someday this stranger
Won't be a stranger
Anymore

Home

AFTER six years of working in a high school for new immigrants, a realization has dawned on me. I am now an immigrant myself. My wife Nikki has accepted a job in Panama City, Panama, for at least a year and we have moved here together. I have taken a leave from my job, and we prepared to leave Minneapolis, Minnesota, almost as if we were preparing to die. We rented out our house, whittled down our material things and put the rest in storage, tied up our affairs, and said goodbye to all of our friends and family. We closed down our lives, at least temporarily. That experience is obviously much different than the experience of the students who I work with, but it has given me a small glimpse of what they might have gone through in their transition to a new country. They became immigrants because of war, political turmoil, or economic reasons. They left their home country because they were hoping for a better life in the United States. We left by our own choice, as they did, but we can buy a ticket, get on a plane and go back any time we feel like it. However, clearly we are committed to living here for the year. My wife has signed a one-year contract for her job here, and we have signed a lease on an apartment until the end of her contract.

There are some things about moving here that quickly became very clear to me. In Panama, I do not have the same rights as I did in the U.S. I cannot vote here and I cannot legally work with a tourist visa. If I want to work, which I do, I have to find a company or school that will sponsor me, or work for cash only, outside the system. Many of the immigrant students I work with have social security numbers because they are legal refugees and have the right to work. But many others do not have a legal right to a job, so they have to work in a situation where the employer does not ask too many questions, or they have to make a false identity. This kind of treatment can make you feel like you are not wanted or welcome in a place, and it is an unpleasant feeling. Shortly after arriving in Panama I interviewed for a job and to my surprise they said they would like me to work for the school, but officially I would be a volunteer. Unofficially they are paying me, in their words, "under the table."

We have now been in Panama for about five months and, honestly, it does not feel like home. When I hear the word home I get sentimental and start to miss the people and lifestyle. The sound of the word brings a great deal of emotional connection with it. Charles Dickens wrote, "Home is a name, a word, it is a strong one; stronger than magician ever spoke, or spirit ever answered to, in the strongest conjuration." Sometimes I feel the transition of making this place our home is gradually starting to happen. It starts to feel very comfortable, like it is becoming familiar. At other times it feels like I am a visitor or foreigner and I start thinking that I want to leave. This surprises me. I thought the adjustment to living here would be much easier for me. I am trying to figure out what makes a place home and when that happens? Is the only place we can call home the place we were born or grew up? It has to be more than that. I think many people truly find homes in their lives that are different places than where they grew up, but that is not such an easy thing to do.

Harriet Beecher Stowe described it like this, "Home is a place not only of strong affections, but of entire unreserve." It is a place where I can do as I like, and fit in just fine. Panama has a good infrastructure and you can find most of the goods and services you need. The people have been great and slowly I am starting to make friends, but I still have a subtle feeling of uneasiness now and then. I think the best way to describe it is that feeling of wanting what you don't have, like the old cliché, "the grass is always greener on the other side." It is human nature to feel that way, so it takes a conscious practice to change it.

More and more I wonder what is really needed to make an existence in life that we can call home. Is home the place you left or the place you are or the place you are going? Emily Dickinson wrote, "Where thou art, that is home." Before I came here I thought the same thing, home is wherever you are living at the time. The philosophy that Dickinson expressed is consistent with the Yoga philosophy of non-attachment and the ability to be content with wherever we find ourselves. In theory I believe it, but now I know that it is something very difficult and challenging to put into practice.

If we have everything we need and more, why does it not feel like home? Oliver Wendell Holmes wrote, "Where we love is home, home that our feet may leave, but not our hearts." In other words, home is the place where you feel a strong emotional attachment. That kind of attachment can take time to develop, probably some years or more. It seems to come much more easily at the place you were raised or experienced major events in your life. On the other hand, I have traveled places for a short period of time and felt a deep connection either because of the people or the place itself. Even with that, I don't feel I could call any of those places home.

By the time we left Panama after living there for a year, I was transformed. I don't know when it switched from only a place to visit to something more, but it clearly did. This was unexpected. Sometime between six and twelve months I reached the point where it felt like it was home. When I returned to Minneapolis, which I thought was home, it was a bit strange. How could two places feel like home? What are the implications if a person can learn to call two different places home? How is it possible? The only thing I can figure out is that it caused me to look at the planet in a different way. Perhaps the whole planet is really our home, not just a particular piece of land. It is one thing to say that, but it is another thing to really experience that.

It gives me some comfort to think of home like this. We are on a journey or trip through life. Everywhere we live is a stop on the itinerary of our lives. Some places we stay longer, some shorter. Wherever we are is the only place we have at the time. None of us know with absolute certainty where we will be in the future. Maybe there will be a surprise like this year when Nikki and I ended up in Panama. I never dreamed that I would be living here, so where I will be living next year could be someplace that I have not even imagined.

The Rock

Born millions of years ago
What has it witnessed
This rock
What shattering changes has it seen
What else will it witness
In the years to come
Long after we are gone
We come and go quickly
Here for only a small fraction of its life
We try not to take it for granted
We exchange pleasantries
Wish it well
Maybe even sit on it
But it does not respond
Or so we think
Seemingly nothing changes
But when does a change become a change
Only when we see it
Or when the rock sees it
When is the unknowable known
When we see it
Or was it there all along
We were just looking the other way

Suddenly I See

WHEN I heard the song by KT Tunstall called "Suddenly I See," I thought, yes, that is how it happens. We learn complicated, new things slowly, and struggle for some time in the process. The new ideas can cause cognitive dissonance while our mind and body try to integrate them. If the new ideas cannot fit into our existing paradigm, a shift must take place. New neural pathways have to be developed. Neuroscientists say that our brain has the innate ability to physically change itself when faced with new and challenging experiences. This ability is called *neuroplasticity*. The latest research says this is true of our brains throughout our entire lives. The brain has the amazing ability to reorganize itself by forming new connections between brain cells (neurons).

How does all of this tie in to our Yoga and Meditation practice? Think back to when you first started practicing Meditation. Do you remember the very first meditation class you attended? Did the concepts seem strange? Beyond the concepts, we were taught that it must be experienced. No one can really explain to you what meditation is. At first it may seem like we don't have the neural pathways or the paradigm to understand it. On the one hand it seemed so familiar and simple, and on the other hand it seemed so complicated and elusive. How is it possible for one concept (like meditation) to be both simple and complicated at the same time? It creates a paradox, a seemingly inconsistent argument. There are many paradoxes we encounter when learning how to meditate. At first, they seem like very foreign concepts that don't fit into our paradigm of how we look at the world. They can create cognitive dissonance. Here are some paradoxes I have encountered through the practice of Meditation:

1. How can you be completely relaxed, yet remain alert, strong and disciplined?
2. How can you be internally focused and externally aware at the same time?
3. How can you watch yourself?
4. How can you let your mind be free and soar and not be daydreaming?
5. What is effortless effort?
6. How do you do more by doing less?
7. How can you be in the present moment and make long term goals?

You can probably think of more meditation paradoxes than this. Many of these questions seem impossible to answer at first. Even after practicing Meditation for many years, the answers are difficult to put into words. It takes a lot of practice for our new neural pathways to develop. And of course the practice has to be done correctly. Then this question arises: How is it possible to practice correctly if we don't know how or what to practice? (Note: Having a good teacher and being initiated is a start.)

Eventually it becomes fruitless to talk or think about it anymore. Too much thinking and talking becomes counterproductive. At some point, we need to put all the techniques aside and realize that the whole process of meditation is very natural. We simply have to begin. Then, someday, when it is least expected, this thought emerges: "Suddenly I See." Suddenly everything comes together, and for a moment, we see. We feel. We perceive that some different state of mind popped up that seems so natural. It seems like it was there all along, but for some reason we couldn't see it. It makes one wonder. What else is out there that we just can't see, but once we see it, we will wonder how we missed it? ✎

For Nikki

On the path of love
And feeling like one
We find strength in a union
Which was only a dream
To renounce a way of living
And take a leap of faith
To trust in someone else
The way you've always trusted in yourself
A window opens
We take the leap
Which seemed so big
For so many years
But land softly
Like a walk in the park
Of comfort, care and concern
Why it happened
We know nothing at all
But when we wake up
We find ourselves together
In a new home
That was there all along

With Gratitude

GRATITUDE. It is a magical, life changing word. It is only one word, but it is so powerful. Learning to live with an attitude of gratitude is a simple, natural, and easy way to bring an immediate positive change into your life. It is the key to opening the door to the seemingly elusive world of joyful living. Everyone would like to bring more joy into their lives. Cultivating more gratitude is a clear path to unlocking this state of mind. Bringing gratitude to one's heart and prayers can immediately make life more positive. It means learning to give thanks for what we have. During especially challenging times it can seem very difficult to do this, but the key is shifting the mind to see things in a little different way. With practice it becomes easier.

Lately, at the end of my Meditation practice, I have started to give thanks for whatever comes to mind. A common theme has been thanking my parents for everything they gave me. Both of my parents have been deceased for many years. But as time goes on and I move through the aging spectrum (I am now fifty-five years old), the perspective I have toward them has changed. It has allowed me to see how they set me up for a nice life through their care and love as I was growing up. Besides the love and care they gave me, I received sufficient experiences and education to allow me to pursue whatever I needed to do in this life. I know they went to great sacrifice to raise me, and I feel directly grateful to them for all that they did. At the end of my Meditation I have started a ritual of giving thanks to them for everything that they did for me. I feel great when I do it.

I also give thanks for anything else that comes into my mind. A recent thought that came into my mind is being thankful for having a meaningful job that allows me to live a comfortable life with the resources I need. For many years I struggled with learning to have a loving attitude toward work. Now I am just starting to realize it is a privilege to go into work every day. Retirement from the job is still probably a few years away, but as it gets closer I can put the work portion of my life in a new and better-understood perspective. Having the opportunity to contribute to the world in a positive way through work is a gift to be cherished.

Often I find myself giving thanks for being born in a time and place that is peaceful, has clean air, clean water, and enough leisure time for spiritual practices like Yoga and Meditation. It is so easy to take this for granted when we live in a place like this day after day and year after year. But how often in history have humans had the opportunity to live this kind of life? I have had fantastic teachers and the time and resources to practice. I don't know if I am learning as much as I could with this opportunity, but I am grateful for being given that chance.

One thing I love to be thankful for is when I arrive home safely after going out into the world. Whether I drive, walk, or bike somewhere, I am so thankful to arrive home. It is a great feeling and I love to give thanks for it. Since I started acknowledging with gratitude this act of arriving home, it has now become a highlight of my day. I simply love to give thanks for this and feel great when I do it.

I don't know why or how this new found attitude of gratitude came to me, but I am grateful for it. It has brought more joy into my life. I did notice that I started giving more thanks at the end of my Meditations at about the same time that Vimala, a friend from The Meditation Center in Minneapolis, went into a hospice situation. While visiting with her recently I told her about the topic of this essay. She said to put this in the essay: "Gratitude is a game-changer." It was clear that moving to an attitude of gratitude allowed her to shift from fear and resentment about her illness to peace, contentment, and acceptance. I had the privilege of spending time with her as the health of her body declined. Her spirit remained high, but I watched her breathing become more and more labored. It reminded me how every smooth, flowing breath I have is a healing gift of relaxation and rejuvenation. As I watched her become more homebound and more dependent on others for her basic needs, it reminded me how nice and pleasant we have it when we are in good health. She passed away during the process of writing this essay, on October 12, 2012. Her passing caused me to realize again how precious and short our visit to the planet is.

Since starting this practice of gratitude, when I finish my twice-daily Meditation practice, many thoughts come into my mind about the various things for which I have to be thankful. These thoughts come naturally and without effort, and I am grateful that they do. I have not listed all the things that I am grateful for in this short essay. The list is endless and keeps growing. One thing I want to be sure and mention is my gratitude about having a loving and supportive wife. No matter what situation in life we find ourselves in, single or married, poor or rich, healthy or not, with or without a job, there is always something to be grateful for. Since I have started the practice of cultivating gratitude I have become a more positive and joyful person. It is an ongoing process, sometimes feeling like it is three steps forward and two steps back. Even with all the challenges of a practice like this, it has definitely been worth the effort. Thank you for taking the time to read this essay!

Writings from *SRIVERM*

DURING the course of writing this book, I realized that we should try to connect it to SRIVERM (www.SRIVERM.net), the school in the remote Himalayas founded by Swami Hari. Judy Law is from Canada and has lived at SRIVERM for most of the last five years. Since all of the profits from the sale of this book will go to SRIVERM, I thought it would be interesting for her to share some of her experiences there.

And of course to hear from the students at SRIVERM is really getting to the heart of the matter. It helps show us more clearly what the funds from the sale of this book really mean to the people who are affected the most.

Story of SRIVERM
by Judy Law

I first entered the fifth grade classroom of SRIVERM in January of 2009, and was met with the bright eyes and smiling innocence of the children waiting for their lesson. The excitement and curiosity they had about a white lady from a different country coming to teach them was plain to see: they could barely contain themselves enough to sit in their seats! For me, I was apprehensive; how and what could I, a stranger to their language and culture, teach them? We were new to each other.

In the Garhwal Himalayan region, in northeast India, daily life is not easy for the people who have settled here. The terrain is very steep, electricity is sporadic, the climate can be harsh for most months of the year, and earning a basic living is an ever-present worry. Most of the population, living in the many small villages that are scattered throughout the hillsides, is poor. The average monthly income for these people is $60 to $75, *if they are fortunate*. But they carry on as best they can, making the most of what little they have. Their resilience in circumstances that would send Westerners running (back to their treasured comforts!) is truly remarkable.

It was these people Swami Hari wanted to help. Many years before the project SRIVERM came into being, Swami Rama had instructed his disciple to help the local people improve their lives through education of the children. Following his Guru's orders, Swami Hari initiated and oversaw construction of a road, school, and guesthouse. In July of 2005 the first classes were in session. Swami Hari told me that it was important that the children of this area, especially the girls, receive a good education. Many of the children in this region drop out of school in the seventh or eighth grade, as their families cannot afford transportation costs. Other reasons children stop their studies are their families' need for help in the fields, tending the goats and cows, and harvesting crops.

In this remote region it is felt by the local people that the best thing for boys is to get accepted into the army (ensuring a steady living); and for girls, to get married. Most villagers do not think beyond this for their children. And if the young man chosen for a young woman to marry is not in the army, she is quite likely to end up with an aimless fellow who passes the time with alcohol. Drinking is a common problem in the mountain regions. The general mentality in this remote region of mountain villages is one of survival, despondency, and, often, hopelessness for a better life.

So, through a good education, Swami Hari wanted to enhance the prospects and expand horizons for the children of this area and their families.

When Swami Hari asked me to be with the children in late 2007 (actually it was more of a demand), I recoiled and replied, "No thanks." I had no background in formal education, and the thought of even attempting to teach without any knowledge of this culture or language was overwhelming to my mind. So how did it happen that I found myself, fourteen months after Swamiji's "request," here in Malethi village, in a classroom before the eager faces of children? And without even the physical, guiding presence of Swami Hari, who had passed away seven months earlier? It seemed I had to jump into this unknown pool. All of my "no, no, and no" had counted for nothing. What else to say about the strange workings of the Guru?

Being in the classroom with the children was a challenge from the start. I was to teach English grammar; but this seemed so trivial to me when I saw students with holes in their too-tight shoes and clothes, and children that were coming to school every day with nothing to eat because their family was too poor to even send a piece of bread. And there were other problems: discipline in the classroom, completion of homework and assignments, concentration and listening skills, proper study habits—all of these were sorely lacking. Some of the students had very low confidence (coming from very poor families and having an abusive home life).

Over the past few years, the poorest students have begun to feel better about themselves; I have felt very happy to see their confidence grow. This shows in their overall improvement in their studies and examinations, and in their increased sense of confidence in the classroom. They are actively participating, where once they sat silent, with eyes downcast, shoulders stooped. Through private donations, these poorest children have tuition, books, clothes and shoes, a hot lunch, and transportation paid for, which eases the family financial burden greatly. All this has given the children, especially the poorest of the poor, a better chance at a good education. But there is still much that is needed on an ongoing basis to ensure a good standard of education in a well-maintained and healthy environment.

Life is truly very simple here, in the Garhwal Himalayas. SRIVERM school serves children from three to thirteen years old, and not one child has a cell phone, iPod, designer clothes, or any of the fancy accessories with which Western kids are so familiar. These children are happy when they receive a new pencil or eraser for a high test score. Because they do not have much of any material "stuff" they are unspoiled and still have much of their innocence and childhood intact. This I have deeply appreciated about them.

In the winters the students and I would be in the classroom fully decked out in our hats, gloves, sweaters, and coats (no heat in the school whatsoever). Whenever it got too cold in the classroom, the other teachers would lay down large blankets on the ground of open areas and we would have our lessons outside in the sun. I often thought that these students, though poor, have the most beautiful view in the world!

Sparrows routinely make their nests in empty light sockets and noisily fly in and out of the classroom. Stray dogs wander in, checking things out and waiting for lunchtime leftovers. The students and teachers take all of this in stride, simply carrying on as though it is the most natural thing.

Over the years I have gradually learned some Hindi, enough to "fool" the students into thinking I know more than I do, which helps to increase my authority in the classroom. But really, it was simply showing up day after day, being there in the classroom with the children, seeing where they needed help, encouragement, or more discipline; and becoming more open to the students showing *me* how to best teach *them*. And with patience, a relationship is developed, a trusting relationship. The students have learned to trust that I follow through with what I say; and I have learned to trust that they are all good kids who deserve a chance to learn and grow fully, and who need time, a heaping dose of patience and positive reinforcement along the way. When there is an openness and willingness of heart, something can be felt that transcends all barriers of nationality, culture, and language. This is what being at this school and with these children has taught me.

Yashi
14 years
SATPULI (TOWN)

The main aim of Swamiji was to educate the poor people of this area. I am proud to be a part of SRIVERM Public School as I have studied here from kindergarten to 8th grade. After completing my studies, my only aim is to be in contact with SRIVERM and I would love to serve the school and the children.

Harsh
12 years
SATPULI

I am happy to be studying in our school because I hope to become a useful human being when I go out of this school. I want to see our school growing day by day and for the name of my school to be known all over.

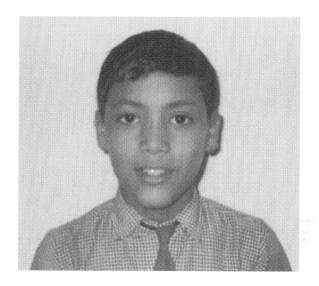

Suraj
12 years
SATPULI

My school teaches me to cultivate better qualities, better habits, and to be a good person. Poor students from far-off villages are also getting the same education at SRIVERM school. I like my school very much.

Srishti
13 years
KHAIRA VILLAGE

My school gives me academic education as well as cultural activities. Imparting knowledge in a comfortable environment is so good for us. That is why I love my school.

Agrima
11 years
GAWANA VILLAGE

I like my school very much because our lessons are very well explained, and all the facilities are available. I feel this is one of the best schools in the state.

Pratibha
12 years
GAWANA VILLAGE

The school is giving so much knowledge to us and I want to give this knowledge to other people also. My school teaches me to stand on my own legs and to be successful in my life. I am proud of my school, and I feel it is the very best school.

Hasidic Tale

ORIGIN UNKNOWN

☙ ❧

THE renowned Hasidic rabbi from Poland, Chofetz Chaim (1838–1933), was visited by an American tourist. The tourist was astonished to see that the rabbi's home was only a simple room, filled with books, plus a table and bench.

"Rabbi," said the tourist, "you are famous and have a large number of students. Where is all your furniture?"

"Where is yours?" replied Chofetz Chaim.

"Mine?" asked the puzzled American. "But I'm only passing through."

"So am I," said the rabbi, "so am I."